EARTH OUR GARDEN HOME

Creation Care Lessons for Children

By Cynthia Coe

Earth Our Garden Home:

Creation Care Lessons for Children

ISBN-13: 978-0692650615 (Sycamore Cove Creations)

ISBN-10: 069265061X

All scripture verses paraphrased by the author.

Published by:

For information, permissions, or to contact the author, please email: info@sycamorecove.org

Contents

An Introduction to Earth Our Garden Home 6

Creation Care Lessons for Children...................9

Lesson One 14

How Does God Care for Creation?

Lesson Two 17

How Does God Feed Us?

Lesson Three 21

Composting as Resurrection

Lesson Four...................24

Living in Harmony with Others

Lesson Five...................27

Proclaim Good News to the Whole Creation

Reflections on the Parables of Jesus 30

Light & Water:

The Parable of the Leaven 32

Seeds & Soil:

The Parable of the Sower 35

Animals:

The Parable of the 39

Jesus as the Gardener:

The Parable of the Mustard Seed 44

Living the Lessons 47

Tips for Making Creation Care a Part of Everyday Life
and Formation

Adding Green Elements to Any Formation Program 47

Mascots & Symbols 49

Crafts, Publicity Materials, and Decorations 50

Snacks 51

Service Projects..52

After Your Program Ends.......................................52

Teaching Creation Care: The Basics 56

The Importance of Special Places in Nature 57

Small Worlds – Looking at the Big Picture, in
Miniature 59

Taking a Closer Look – Mapping and Drawing 60

Mapping and Drawing as Metaphors of Life in
Christ 62

Using Your Church and Grounds to

Teach Creation Care 64

Play Areas and Classrooms 65

Going Off the Grid 67

Acknowledgements...71

About the Author..73

Resources for Teaching 75

and Studying Creation Care

An Introduction to

Earth Our Garden Home
Creation Care Lessons for Children

Who should use these resources?

Church leaders, clergy, Christian educators, parents, and young people are invited to use these resources to grow and develop in stewardship of God's creation and in their own personal spirituality through these resources. These resources may be used with faith-based summer camp programs, vacation Bible school programs, and schools.

What resources are included in Earth Our Garden Home?

This collection of resources includes:

- 5 *Creation Care Lessons*, based on scripture and offering an experiential game, follow-up discussion questions, and a prayer

- *Reflections on the Parables of Jesus*, offering alternate wondering questions and background information to look at several parables through a creation care lens (for use with Montessori based Christian formation programs)

- *Living the Lessons*, tips and suggestions for adding creation care to an existing Christian formation program and for incorporating creation care into children's home, school, and church life

What is new and different about these resources?

These resources were developed using best practices of environmental education. Almost all of the exercises, lessons, and even worship experiences are highly experiential for the participants. They are best carried out in nature itself, whether a wilderness area, a camp, or simply a church garden or urban park. Creation care is best learned outdoors, in nature and personally experienced. If you get people outdoors, much of your lesson is already in progress. If outdoor lesson time is not feasible, you may easily adapt these lesson plans to indoor use.

Do I have to use all these resources? Am I free to pick and choose from these resources?

You are absolutely welcome to use these resources as you see fit! Faith leaders and formation directors seeking to introduce creation care to their congregations are free to pick

7

and choose activities that will best serve their groups and context.

What about applying these concepts in real life?

An important factor to keep in mind is follow-up and transfer of learning. It's great to present these concepts and conduct exercises in environmental stewardship, but it's far most important that participants are given the means and the inspiration to act upon these ideas in their daily lives and out in the world. The final section of these resources, *Living the Lessons*, provides tips and suggestions for adding creation care to existing programs and for follow-up in children's homes, schools, and church life.

Creation Care Lessons for Children

Earth Our Garden Home

Creation Care Lessons For Children

This collection of lessons introduces children to the connections between faith and the natural world. Children are introduced to the concept that all we have ultimately comes from God through the gifts of the natural world. All of creation is connected – much like the Body of Christ – as each plant or animal depends upon other elements of the natural world for its own survival.

Each lesson includes:

- A short verse of scripture from the Bible
- A game or activity
- Follow-up questions to enhance and reinforce learning
- A prayer.

You are welcome to use these lessons independently, as a complete unit, or to supplement or enhance an existing program.

These lessons also introduce concepts of wise stewardship of natural resources and care of God's creation. Children are introduced to the cycle of life and the concept of sustainability as ways they participate in the continuing process of creation in our world. By learning to compost and be mindful of where waste products go, children can learn to live in harmony with God's creation and to actively participate in this process of sustainability. These concepts introduce to children the concept of stewardship by focusing on where our food, clothing, and other materials come from. Children are encouraged to think about how they might best use these precious resources – many of which may be irreplaceable if not used wisely or sustainably.

Finally, issues of social justice are introduced by asking children to consider how their use of land and natural resources affects their immediate neighbors. By asking children to look beyond their own personal uses of resources – and by considering where waste products go – children might begin to think of how all human use of resources affects other humans in some way. Wellness issues are introduced as well, as children look at food sources in their own neighborhoods and are encouraged to make use of locally grown food – or even grow food themselves.

A joy of introducing these concepts of sustainability, social justice, and wellness to young children is that they usually "get" these concepts very easily. Young children naturally love nature and want to be a part of it. Children easily understand concepts involving sharing, treating others with consideration, and treating all of creation with care and kindness. By talking about these issues and intentionally making them a part of our Christian faith, we hope these children will retain this love and care of nature – and each other – for the rest of their lives.

Tips for Using These Lessons:

- Hold classes outside, if at all possible
- Let children freely roam outdoors as much as possible, setting boundaries in advance
- Ask children to work in pairs or small groups to enhance safety
- Ask adult leaders to keep an eye on specific zones assigned to each adult while outdoors (rather than congregating and chatting with each other)
- Have a simple first aid kit handy (band aids, wipes, a cell phone for emergencies)

- In discussing where food comes from with small children, you might refrain from discussing the gory details of butchering animals for meat. You might simply say, "bacon comes from pigs."

A Note About Scripture Verses:

All scripture verses have been paraphrased to be more conversational and accessible to young children. Teachers are encouraged to tell these stories in their own words and without notes, if possible.

Lesson One

How Does God Care for Creation?

Scripture: Luke 12:22 & 27

Think about birds, like the ravens. These birds neither sow seeds nor reap any harvest. They have no barn nor any kind of storehouse. Yet God feeds them.

Think about flowers like the lilies. Think about how they grow. They don't do any work. They don't spin any kind of cloth to make their magnificent clothes. Yet King Solomon in all his glory was not clothed as beautifully as these flowers.

How does God feed creatures and other living things in our world?

Game: God Feeds All Creatures

Find something in nature that feeds something else.

- Divide group into pairs or small groups
- Within a designated area, find and name something that feeds another plant or creature. (Small children may draw; older kids may draw or list.)
- Bonus points for finding a water source.
- Everyone wins! Each group or pair gets a prize (a healthy snack or drink or something made of sustainable materials)

Follow-up and Focus:

Ask children these questions to enhance learning and focus on the main points of the scripture:

- How does God feed all the creatures and plants we found?
- How are all the plants and animals connected to each other?
- How are all these plants and animals like the ravens, depending on God to feed them?
- What did the Bible verse mean, when it said a great king in all his glory was not clothed like a simple flower?
- What does the beauty of flowers tell us about God?

- How does the beauty of flowers and plants help us know God better?

Prayer: We thank you, Lord, for the beauty of all nature. We thank you for rocks, soil, water, all plants, and all animals. Help us to know you through the beauty of nature. Help us to understand you better through the interconnectedness of all creation. Help us to care for your creation as you care for the Body of Christ that is all of us. In Christ's name, Amen.

Lesson Two

**How Does God
Feed Us?**

Scripture: Luke 12:28 - 31

If God takes care of the grass of the field – even though it is alive today and thrown into the oven tomorrow – how much more will God take care of you! Don't worry about what you will eat and what you will drink. The nations of the world worry about such things, and God knows that you need them. But instead of worrying about what you will eat and drink, strive for the Kingdom of God, and these things will be given to you as well.

How does our environment feed and sustain us?

Game: A Watershed Moment

If we had to feed and support ourselves from this land alone, how would we do that?

- Ask children to name all elements of nature they see in a certain area. This area should be large enough to include enough land for a garden. If possible, the availability of a water source and assets such as trees, rocks, and even domesticated animals will enhance this lesson.

- Parts of nature useful for human survival may be listed on cards or on a large bulletin board or dry erase board. Younger children might also draw their responses on a large sheet of paper.

- Dividing children in small groups or pairs, ask each group to use their imaginations to come up with a plan for living on this land. They might pretend they are pioneers, settlers, or even people from another country or planet who have landed in this place and need to keep themselves alive.

- For younger children, "loose objects" such as small wooden tree limbs or logs might be provided so that children might build a fort and plan a settlement.

Children might also draw a picture of their plan for survival, plan a skit, or make a diorama.

Follow-up and Focus: Ask children these questions to enhance learning and focus on the main points of the scripture:

- What gifts of creation did you find on the land to help you and your group live?
- What did you do to get these gifts?
- Does anyone in our world today live on the land without worrying about where their food, clothing, and shelter come from? How are they able to do this?
- Who helps you get food, clothing, and shelter? How is your food, clothing, and shelter a gift from God's creation?
- What would it mean for your family to "strive for the kingdom of God" instead of worrying about how your needs will be met? What would need to happen for you to do this?

Prayer: We thank you, Lord, for feeding us, clothing us, and giving us shelter through all the gifts of your creation. Help us to appreciate, every day, all these gifts that help us to live on this beautiful earth. Help us to use the gifts from your creation to strive for the kingdom of God, both in our own lives and in the lives of others. In Christ's name, Amen.

Lesson Three

**Composting
as Resurrection**

Scripture: John 12:24

This is a truth told by Jesus: when a grain of wheat falls to earth, it remains nothing more than just a single grain of wheat. But if it is dies and is buried in the earth, it germinates and grows into a new plant that provides food for other creatures.

How can we live our lives sustainably, helping new creation to take place continually?

Game - Will it Compost?

- Bring in scraps from snack or breakfast OR use photographs of meals.
- Go over "rules" of what can be composted and what cannot be composted.

  uncooked fruits and veggies – yes

  paper and leaves – yes

  meat and diary products – no

  cooked food or processed foods – no
- In teams or pairs, identify what is compostable and what is not; award points for each good answer.
- As an additional activity – children might construct and begin composting in a bin for their parish, home, or school.

Follow-up and Focus:

Ask children these questions to enhance learning and focus on the main points of the scripture:

- How can composting provide new life?
- What other ways can we re-use household, school, or church materials to give them new life?
- How does giving new life to these materials help care for God's creation?
- In what ways does new life on earth depend on us?

Prayer: We thank you, Lord, for the gift of new life on earth. Help us to care for your creation in ways that nourishes and protects the cycle of life on earth. Help us to use our resources wisely and in ways that honor the many natural gifts that you have given us. Help us to live in harmony with your creation, in our daily lives and in all we do. In Christ's name, Amen.

Lesson Four

Living in Harmony with Others

Scripture – Matthew 7:12

This is one of the most important teachings Jesus gave us: Behave towards others as you would want them to behave towards you.

How does the Golden Rule apply to care of God's creation?

Sustainability can sometimes mean taking the time and effort to do something difficult, instead of doing something easy and convenient – especially if this affects others.

Game – Where Does it Go?

- Make a list or draw all of the items that will eventually leave your church building, school, or home. Don't forget water, emissions from heat sources, papers, trash, and even sewage. Older children might also examine any pesticides, herbicides, or other chemicals used.

- Assign a pair or team of children to each item or to a group of items. Ask them to think about where the item or group of items will eventually go.

- Teams might draw a map of where their item or group of items go after the materials leave the building.

- Children may need help from adults or more information for this exercise to learn about landfills, water treatment plants, recycling plants, and other disposal sites. Information sheets on each of these sites might be prepared and given to children to match to the items assigned.

Follow Up and Focus:

Ask children these questions to enhance learning and focus on the main points of the scripture:

- Who lives near these disposal sites?
- Who comes in contact with these materials once they leave the building or grounds?
- Are some people more affected by disposal of these materials than others?
- Would you want to live near places where these materials end up?
- How can we dispose of materials in a way that shows kindness and respect to others?

Prayer: We thank you, Lord, for all of the earth and for all peoples who live on this earth. Help us to see all people as neighbors. Help us to treat all others with the kindness, respect, and dignity with which we would want to be treated ourselves. Help us to live in harmony with all other people and with your creation. In Christ's name, Amen.

Lesson Five

**Proclaim Good News
to the Whole Creation**

Scripture: Mark 16:15

Jesus gave us this command: Go out into the world and take the good news to all of creation.

How do we take "good news" to all of creation? How can we spread good news of healthier, sustainable living to others?

Game: Who Could You Tell?

This is an exercise in "walking the walk" and "talking the talk."

- Working in pairs or teams, children share what "good news" of creation care they could give to others.

- Each child picks one person they know, one region of the world, OR a favorite plant or animal.

- Each child then shares "good news" of what humans can do to make life better for that person, region, plant, or animal.

- Children may also draw pictures to share this good news or prepare a bulletin board or other display to share good news of creation care with your church, school, or community.

Follow Up and Focus:

Ask children these questions to enhance learning and focus on the main points of the scripture:

- What can you do each day that could show care for all creation?

- Is it better to talk about care of creation, or to do something to care for creation, or both?

- How do you think others will respond to your good news?

- What would happen if this good news spread to the whole creation?

- When and how will you share good news of creation care after our time together ends?

Prayer: Thank you, Lord, for the opportunity to share good news with the whole creation. Help us to not only tell others about care of your creation, but to show others the importance of creation care for all life on earth. Help us to love your creation as you love us, caring for the whole earth as you care for us. In Christ's name, Amen.

Reflections on the Parables of Jesus

These reflections on the Parables of Jesus are designed for use with smaller children, particularly those in Montessori Christian formation programs. Bright, colorful, hands-on pictures of the elements of these parables open up the scriptures to new and relevant meaning through visual and kinesthetic cues. Even if children are already familiar with these parables, seeing the parables in the context of creation care will deepen their understanding of both the scriptures and of creation care.

30

Reflection and Background materials are provided to assist adult leaders and teachers in preparing for their lessons or presentations. Teachers may use all or parts of this background material in their presentations to children. These materials may also be used with intergenerational groups.

The Parables of Jesus are masterpieces of teaching tools, suitable and accessible for all ages and stages of human beings. In these readings, the "pieces" of the parables – soil, seeds, animals and human characters – are seen in a literal framework, rather than the figurative framework often used by people of faith.

For an added environmental dimension to your presentation, these parables could be presented outdoors, on the ground, in a garden, or in the grass. Sounds from birds and even visits from insects will enhance your presentation and emphasize the connection between these scripture passages and the earth.

Light & Water:

The Parable of the Leaven

Scripture: Matthew 13:33

The Kingdom of Heaven is like the process of making bread. A woman takes yeast and mixes it with three measures of flour. She mixes the yeast with the flour until the mixture is all leavened.

Background and Reflection for Adults:

In this parable, the means of fermentation – the "leaven" – is yeast. The process of fermentation is not a particular pretty subject, but across cultures, this is an important means of transforming raw grain, fruits, vegetables, meats, and even dairy products into food we can eat.

The woman in the parable would likely have gotten this leaven by putting a stale piece of bread in a dark, damp place until mold formed. She also may have gotten this yeast from a neighbor who shared it with her. These "behind the scene" facts open up more depth to the parable, simply by challenging us to look at where one of the "pieces" of the story – the leaven – came from.

We can also look at the grain and water in this story in the same literal way. Where did they come from? How did they get to this woman's home before becoming part of the bread she would serve to her family, share with neighbors, or serve to complete strangers?

When bread is made, the bread maker mixes wheat flour with a relatively small amount of water and a tiny portion of yeast. Yet after this mixture is set aside for a period of time, often covered by a cloth and out of sight, a marvelous process takes place. The mixture expands, becoming a big, gooey blob of dough far larger and airier than the compact and fairly flat concoction first mixed together in a small bowl.

These processes of nature happen all around us, all the time, and often in darkness and out of sight. Many of the "processes" of life on earth – including the process of growth – similarly takes place quietly and often unacknowledged and perhaps unappreciated.

Questions for Reflection:

- I wonder where the flour came from? Who grew the wheat? Who harvested it? Who sold it to the woman?

- I wonder how she paid for the flour? I wonder where the water came from? I wonder how the water got into the woman's home?

- I wonder where the leaven came from?

- I wonder if we need periods of dark and light for all our food?

- I wonder if we need water for most – or even all – of our food?

- I wonder if everyone needs light and water for their food? I wonder what would happen if we didn't have the sun and water?

- I wonder where the food and drink we eat for our snack today comes from? I wonder who grew it, baked it, and brought it to us? I wonder where the water in our drinks comes from?

- I wonder if we are all connected by water and by sunlight?

- I wonder if we can help everyone have clean water and live in the light?

Seeds & Soil:

The Parable of the Sower

Scripture: Matthew 13:3-9

Listen to this story told by Jesus: A farmer went out to sow seeds. Some seeds fell on a path, and birds came along and ate them up. Other seeds fell on rocky ground, where there was not much soil. The seeds sprang up quickly, since the soil was so shallow. But the sun scorched the seeds, and since they were so poorly rooted, the seedlings withered away. Other seeds feel among thorns, but the thorns grew up around them and choked the seedlings. Yet more seeds fell into good soil, and they produced grain – some a hundredfold, some sixtyfold, some thirtyfold of what the farmer sowed. Anyone with ears should listen to this story!

Background and Reflection for Adults:

This parable is usually about abundant harvest for people and the ministry of the church. But we can also think about care of the earth in this parable. If you look at the four scenarios in this story – the path, the rocky soil, the thorn patch, and the "good soil" – you are actually looking at four types of soil humans regularly encounter. Part of our land is used for travel and is trod on without attention to agriculture (though in this story, the birds get to eat the seeds spread there). Parts of the earth are rocky, but these rocks erode to become part of soil where plants will grow. Much of the earth is still wilderness or semi-wilderness, where wildflowers like thistles with sharp thorns grow. And of course, some of our land is the "good soil" where we grow crops to feed ourselves and domesticated animals. If we look at all these types of land, we see that all of them are important in producing either nutrients or oxygen for our agricultural use – or to help get crops to market.

In examining the concept of "good soil" in this parable, it is helpful to know something about what makes soil "good" and what is needed to sustain plant growth. Good soil needs nutrients – specifically nitrogen, phosphorus, and potassium – to nourish seeds. Seeds also need warmth, air and water to germinate, with proper drainage to carry away excess water. Much of this nutrition comes from other plants that have died and become compost. Rocks and sand also make up good soil. All of these elements (except, interestingly, water) are portrayed in this parable, and thinking about these elements in their literal sense opens up to us many issues connected to environmental stewardship.

Questions for Reflection:

- I wonder what kind of seeds the sower planted?
- I wonder if he knew the birds would eat the seeds?
- I wonder why the sower spread seeds on rocks and among the thorns?
- I wonder if any other creatures ate the seeds?
- I wonder what kind of plants had those thorns? I wonder what creatures lived among the thorns?
- I wonder what happened to the plants that withered away?
- I wonder how the good soil got to be so good?
- I wonder where the water for the soil came from?
- I wonder how we get "good soil" for the plants we eat?
- I wonder what would happen if we didn't have soil for paths, for thorns, or if we didn't have rocky places?

- I wonder what the sower will do with all those seeds in the harvest bags?
- I wonder who this sower is?

Animals:

**The Parable of the
Good Shepherd**

Scripture: Psalm 23:1-4; John 10:11-16; Luke15:3-7

When people asked Jesus who he was, he told them, I am the Good Shepherd. I know my sheep, and my sheep know me. I lead my flock to still waters and green pasture. A good shepherd lays down his life for his sheep.

If one of my sheep is lost, I will leave my flock in the wilderness and go after it until I find it. When I find the lost sheep, I will put it on my shoulders and rejoice.

An ordinary shepherd does not care for the sheep like the Good Shepherd. If a wolf comes, an ordinary shepherd leaves the sheep alone and runs away. The wolf then snatches the sheep and scatters them.

39

Background and Reflection for Adults:

The "parable" of the Good Shepherd actually draws imagery from both the Twenty-third Psalm and the Gospels of the New Testament. The image of Jesus as the Good Shepherd is one of comfort, helping us to know that God provides for our basic needs, leads us back to safety when we are lost, and guides us through the dark places in our lives. This imagery is often a central concept presented to children, as it provides rich but easily accessible material for reflection on the nature of God.

In environmental terms, this parable also provides rich material for reflection. As we imagine the Good Shepherd leading to green pastures and clear, cool water, we might wonder how - as the hands and feet of Christ - we might lead others to the rich nutrition of green fields and clean water. We might reflect on how we might help find the lost who do not enjoy lovely pastures and clean water in their communities. We might wonder how we might truly act as though humans are indeed "one flock," all of whom need pastures and clean water to survive.

In terms of the wolf in this story, these scripture passages might be seen as a reflection on differences between domesticated and wild animals. While we usually see the wolf in this story as a figure of evil, we might now think of the wolf as the presence of "wilderness" in our world. Wolves are every bit part of God's creation as sheep. Wolves need to eat, too, and are actually indicators of an environment healthy enough to support large mammals. Just as we saw St. Francis convince a wolf to live in harmony with a human community, we might reflect on how we can both provide a healthy and harmonious environment for all animals, both wild and domestic.

The "ordinary shepherd" is also an interesting but usually overlooked figure in the Good Shepherd imagery. In our time, we might see the "ordinary shepherd" as a typical person who goes along with the crowd and treats the environment with the same benign neglect as most other people. If he or she is not directly affected by an environmental disaster, the environment is taken for granted, given little thought, and treated without regard for consequences of small actions. Our challenge is to rise above this benign neglect and to actively care for the environment, as would a Good Shepherd.

Questions for Reflection:

- I wonder how the Good Shepherd knows how to find the good grass? I wonder what makes the grass "good?"

- I wonder what other creatures eat this grass or even live in this grass?

- I wonder how the Good Shepherd finds the clear, clean water? I wonder what the Shepherd would do if he could not find clean water for the sheep?

- I wonder if other animals need clear, clean water?

- I wonder if other animals live in this water?

- I wonder what these dark places really are?

- I wonder if anything lives in these dark places?

- I wonder if the Good Shepherd is afraid of these dark places?

- I wonder if we have dark places in our world? I wonder what they would be?

- I wonder how hard the Good Shepherd had to look to find the lost sheep? I wonder why this sheep was so important to him?

- I wonder if the shepherd has other animals? I wonder if he cares about those animals, too?

- I wonder if we could find good grass and clean water for our own animals? I wonder what we would do if we couldn't find good grass and clean water for them?

Additional Reflection Questions

- I wonder who this ordinary shepherd is?

- I wonder why he doesn't take care of the sheep?

- I wonder if the sheep find food and water on their own?

- I wonder why there is a wolf in this story?

- I wonder what the wolf needs to eat and drink?

- I wonder why the wolf does not attack the Good Shepherd? I wonder why the Good Shepherd doesn't attack the wolf?

- I wonder why there is a wolf in this story?

- I wonder what this story is really about?

Jesus as the
Gardener:

The Parable of the
Mustard Seed

**Scripture*:* Luke 13:18-19

People asked Jesus what the Kingdom of God is like. Jesus compared the Kingdom of God to a mustard seed. He said the Kingdom of God is like a mustard seed that someone takes and sows in the garden. The seed grows and becomes a tree, and birds make their nests in its branches.

Background and Reflection for Adults:

This parable is about a mustard seed. The mustard seed Jesus talks about in this parable is much smaller than the mustard seeds we might have in our spice cabinets at home. It is so small, that it looks like a tiny black speck. Yet when it grows, it becomes one of the largest shrubs on earth. It is so large, it is taller than a house.

The type of mustard seed Jesus would have known is also highly invasive. To import this seed into the United

44

States, this type of mustard seed must be irradiated first, so that it will not cause environmental problems on this continent.

This parable is usually told to explore how the Kingdom of God spreads. We can also think of how "seeds" of inspiration and examples of good environmental stewardship can also begin with our words and deeds. We can think about how "seeds" of knowledge, imagination, and ideas have been planted in us, and how we these seeds might grow throughout our community and the world.

Children almost always associate the "Sower" of the mustard seed with Jesus, and we, too, can think of Jesus the Gardener – as he appeared to the women who first witnessed his resurrection outside the tomb. If Jesus is seen as the Gardener, how might this change our view of Earth, our garden home? As the hands and feet of Christ, how might we sow seeds of creation in our lives and on Earth, our Common Home?

Questions for Reflection:

- I wonder why the Sower put the seed in this garden? I wonder what he hoped would happen?
- I wonder how the tree grew? I wonder what nourished it and helped it to grow?

- I wonder what the birds thought of this tree? I wonder where they would have put their nests if the Sower had not planted this seed?

- I wonder what the people who live near this tree think about it?

- I wonder what seeds have been planted in us?

- I wonder what will nourish them and help them to grow?

- I wonder what these seeds will grow into?

- I wonder if those seeds will help birds and other animals build their nests or homes?

- I wonder if those seeds can be shared in other gardens?

- I wonder what this garden really is?

Living the Lessons

Tips for Making Creation Care a Part of Everyday Life and Formation

Adding Green Elements to Any Formation Program

Care of creation may be added to any existing program for young people. By adding plants, flowers, or other all-natural elements to what you are already doing, you can make a small but important statement about the importance of the natural world. Even if you don't talk about the beauty of the world, you can embrace this concept by holding classes outdoors or – if that's not feasible – bringing more of the outdoors into our programs. Greening our worship spaces and classrooms with the beauty of the earth goes a long way towards demonstrating what is important in our programs for young people.

We can also incorporate Creation Care in our outreach programs. Whether we are feeding the hungry, tutoring children living in poverty, building housing, or working for social justice, we can embrace and demonstrate creation care by the products we buy, the materials we use, and by what we do with our waste. Feeding programs can utilize compost bins, educational programs can incorporate recycling activities, and social justice efforts can make sure they "walk the walk" environmentally alongside their journeys towards justice.

Whether we want to admit it or not, environmental stewardship touches every ministry in the church. And our young people watch us to set examples. Whether it's use of transportation, choice of food to serve at church dinners, use of cups that can't be recycled or reused during the parish coffee hour after church, or excessive use of craft materials, we show young people in our churches what we value and what kind of stewards we are. If we want young people to grow into good stewards of their resources, we have to model good behavior ourselves in our daily ministries.

In any program for young people, what you do and how you act often speaks louder than anything you say. In environmental educational programs in particular, children and youth may indeed learn as much or more from the details of how your program is carried out than the actual "lessons." For these reasons, you might take a hard look at the details of your program and make sure that they "fit" with what you hope to teach.

Here are ways you might work creation care into your formation ministry:

Mascots & Symbols – Many programs use pictures of a "mascot" or other visual symbol to name each age group (e.g. "the rainbows," "the stars," "the comets,"). Consider using animals or plants native to your community or region to help children get to know and appreciate the wildlife that shares the land around them. (For instance, small groups could be called "the bears," "the squirrels," "the blue jays," or the "golden rain trees.")Young people might even choose a mascot themselves by doing research on the internet or in a field guide, so they might learn something about the animal or plant and its characteristics. They could even develop a team cheer, make t-shirts or name tags, or make a flag showing their chosen mascot.

Crafts, Publicity Materials, and Decorations – Children might learn more about reducing, re-using, and recycling from what they see church leaders do than any lesson you might give them. These unspoken "lessons" in use of resources may set examples that could carry over into home life - even for the rest of their lives.

As you choose ways to publicize, communicate to parents, and decorate your teaching space, consider how you can use sustainable and re-used or re-usable materials. Digital communications and use of social media might save a lot of paper that would otherwise go to the landfill. If your program takes place outside, the beauty of the land may be all the "decoration" you need.

Similarly, in choosing craft activities, consider using sustainable materials – or even natural materials thoughtfully gathered from your local area (wood, leaves, vines, rocks). Crafts can become lifelong activities providing young people with a quiet, enjoyable and even meditative experience. True crafts also produce useful items, much like people in earlier times handmade items to use in their daily lives. Consider teaching crafts that might "stick" with young people in years to come, and give them the opportunity to make something they or their families will actually use (instead of throw away the moment your program ends).

Finally, as your time with young people concludes, make sure recyclable materials are put in a bin for recycling or re-used in some way. Make sure young people are involved in this process, as a means of one last lesson in creation care.

Snacks – The food served to young people can send an important message of what your faith community values. To reflect your community's focus on wellness, healing, and good stewardship, make sure snacks and drinks served to young people reflect this focus. Fresh cut, organically grown fruit makes a terrific snack anyone can enjoy. If you are able to provide locally grown fruits or vegetables for a snack, all the better. (You might even ask the local farmer to join you for a visit or go visit the place where snacks are grown.)

Even if you choose to serve cookies or another snack with more calories, you might serve fruit first and wait a few minutes for children to have a chance to eat this healthy snack before serving something else. You might be surprised at how popular fruit can be with children if it's the only snack served or in sight.

If you choose cookies or crackers for a snack, buying in bulk and reducing excess packaging is an important way you can "walk the walk" of environmental stewardship (and save money at the same time). Also, consider what happens with leftovers and trash resulting from snacks or any food service you offer. Fresh fruits and vegies should go to a compost bin. Packaging, plates, and any utensils should be recycled.

Service Projects – Many faith communities offer one or more service projects in which children and young people may participate. A wealth of opportunities involve good environmental stewardship. You might raise money to plant trees in an area of your community, plant trees or flowers on your church property, start a recycling program for your church, or collect money for an international relief or development agency offering programs to help with organic farming, reforestation, clean water, sanitation, or clean energy. You might even support programs both in your own community and overseas, to show our common environmental link with communities all over the world.

After Your Program Ends – An important part of any educational program is "transfer of learning" – the process of making the lesson "stick" with learners and become part of everyday life. There are several ways you can help young people retain what they learn about environmental stewardship long after your time with them ends:

- Provide a "starter kit" of leaves, paper, and fruit and vegie left-overs for a home compost project.

- Offer time and space for young people to plan a home recycling program.

- Offer digital or paper "badges" on a continuing basis for environmental stewardship projects completed at home.

- Offer opportunities to plant a small mini-garden to take home and care for.

- Post regular environmental stewardship tips and reminders in your faith community's monthly or weekly communications; include young people's ongoing efforts.

- Include wellness and social justice issues touching environmentalism in adult programs attended by parents, and ask parents to share what they learn and what they think about these issues with their children.

- Recommend resources, books, articles, and online posts on environmental stewardship to your faith community. (A full list of resources is available at the end of this book.)

Include the Parents

Including Parents and other caregivers or family members in the theme and content of your camp is a great way to get entire families on board with environmental stewardship. It is not unheard of for children to go home from school or camp, eager to start a home recycling program and able to convince otherwise reluctant parents to join in.

Also, children and youth are apt to put parents on a "need to know" basis as to their school and camp activities. By providing a showcase of camp activities and good follow-up communications, camp leaders may give parents and caregivers a full picture of your camp program and what their children did during the week. Offering a handout highlighting the themes and content of your program – via paper or digitally – can also help parents and caregivers follow up and participate with their children in new environmental stewardship efforts, such as home energy saving measures or recycling efforts. As an alternative, campers might give tours of their activities to parents or caregivers who come to pick them up.

Leave No Trace

An important part of camp is cleaning up. Be sure to include the campers themselves in this effort! Cleaning up and preparing for others to use the land and facilities is an important part of environmental stewardship...as well as an important last lesson of your program.

Any land used for "forts" or "special places" built by children or youth should be restored to its natural condition. Children may be reluctant to dismantle these special places, but part of environmental stewardship includes consideration for those coming after us, allowing them the same enjoyment of the land that we have enjoyed ourselves. Children might be encouraged to say a prayer of thanks for their special place or have a "decommissioning ceremony" for their fort or special place before dismantling.

Teaching Creation Care: The Basics

Children and youth learn much through simply being members of families, communities, and faith groups. Creation care may largely be "taught" in faith communities by making children and youth part of any environmental stewardship projects the church might involve itself in. If your church starts a recycling project by putting out bins for paper, plastic, and aluminum waste, make sure children and teens are asked to participate. If you add solar panels to the roof or buy an electric car for your clergy, make sure you tell kids about this...and tell them why these actions were taken by your church.

But simply making children a part of environmental stewardship practices is not quite enough. In a culture where many adults did not grow up with a good sense of creation care as a faith practice, we need to be more intentional about explicitly and deliberately teaching creation care as part of Sunday School and other faith formation programs.

In the secular world, a huge amount of research has been done in recent years to determine how best to teach environmental studies. We can now point to best practices of environmental education and use these best practices in Christian formation programs offered to children and youth. Some of these techniques are basic common sense, such as just plain getting children outside more. Other techniques are completely compatible with spiritual disciplines we already practice in Christianity, such as drawing flowers and leaves as a quiet, calming means of noticing the magnificent design and complexity of natural elements or quiet walks or hikes in nature. Other techniques open the door for new and fun ways of using church resources to teach Christian formation...and to practice good stewardship of our resources as well.

The Importance of Special Places in Nature

Developing a "sense of "place" within nature is a part of childhood that can stay with us for a lifetime. Becoming attached to a particular spot in nature can also motivate children to later become aware and concerned about environmental issues. This sense of place is not something that can be learned from a book; a sense of place is developed from personal experience.

Though adults can also develop a sense of place, the freedom and curiosity of children is an optimum time to develop an attachment to both special places in nature and to the overall environment itself. Did you build a "fort" outside when you were a child? You were not alone in this experience. Building forts, treehouses, and other special places outdoors is a universal tendency among children, particularly between the ages of seven and twelve. Special places like forts can serve as a home-away-from-home in nature, serving as a bridge between protected family life and the wider world of adolescence. Special places help children bond with nature, feel comfortable in it, and become committed to acting as caretakers and stewards of nature later in life.

To make a special place in nature truly their own, young people need to be able to arrange, re-arrange, and build their special places themselves. In camp situations, adult supervisors or counselors may of course set necessary boundaries or parameters. But children should have the freedom to select an area for their special place, move around logs and rocks, and make the place their own.

An availability of "loose objects" is important - a wide variety of leaves, sticks, wood stumps, stones, and even water. These objects help children tap into their creativity and inventiveness, further allowing them to discover the wonder and pure fun of playing outdoors.

In introducing faith closely linked with nature, teens and adults might be invited to find a "special place" in nature as well. This special place – a quiet bench in a park, a garden, or simply a porch with a lovely view – could serve as a place to pray, meditate, journal, or even have a small group discussion or Bible study. This time in nature could foster healing and spirituality, allowing busy teens and adults time to take a break from the demands of the world, get in touch with their true selves, and listen to God.

Small Worlds – Looking at the Big Picture, in Miniature

An activity that can help children understand the world around them is an opportunity to make a "small world" for themselves. This "small world" can take the form of a diorama, a miniature scale model of an area, or even a terrarium or miniature garden.

Making a small world gives children a chance to look at the big picture of an area, yet in a way that is manageable and understandable to the child. If the area is a town or urban area, the child is able to look at infrastructure, waste disposal systems, transportation systems, food supply systems, and patterns that impact the way people live. If the area is an all-natural scene, the child is able to examine the smaller parts that make up the whole, such as a water supply, drainage, the availability of sunlight and shade, and the availability of nutritious soil.

Small World activities also give children a relatively calm and creative space in which to play or work. When taken home, the small world may become a small part of nature the child feels responsibility for caring for. When a child cares for just one small part of nature, the child is more likely to care for the entire environment as an adult.

Taking a Closer Look – Mapping and Drawing

Too often, our modern world tends to look only at buildings, major highways, shopping centers, and other man-made structures in describing our environment. We miss the awesomely amazing world of nature we pass through every day - a nature that has stories to tell, an ancient past, an ever-changing profile, and which affects the way we live our lives. As faith leaders, we may need to begin our introduction to creation care by asking young people to first take a closer look at the world around them.

Mapping is a technique used in secular environmental education that can be utilized in Christian formation programs to help children and youth develop a greater sense of environmental stewardship. Making a map of a piece of the environment helps young people notice detailed features of a landscape, including features of plants, animal habitats, and topography they may have overlooked in simply passing through an area. Mapping also helps young people feel rooted, connected, and comfortable in a place.

Maps may be constructed from very simple and inexpensive materials. Maps may be made on a simple sheet of large construction paper or butcher paper, using markers, colored pencils, or crayons. Exact scale or distances are not important; the point of the exercise is for young people to notice special features of the landscape. Encourage children to map and label trees, large rocks or boulders, water features like creeks or springs, along with low places and high places like hills or cliffs. Mapping other features defining the land – soil type, plant life, animal nests or tracks, human structures – will open children's eyes to the true complexity and marvels of the land around them.

Drawing is another way to introduce the marvelous complexity and design of God's creation. Like mapping, drawing invites children (and adults) to a quiet time of closely examining a flower, a leaf, or even something larger and more complex, like a tree or mountain stream. Artistic competence is not the point. The point is to invite young people to take time to really and truly look at the magnificent intricacy and beauty of God's creation. In sitting down to attempt to draw the texture, structure, and color of even one simple flower, we are able to better appreciate with wonder and awe the gift of creation.

As an alternative, youth might also use digital cameras or their phones to photograph flowers, plants, or other parts of nature that interest or "speak" to them. Like drawing, taking the time to look closely at nature leads to deeper appreciation of the natural world in which we live.

Mapping and Drawing as Metaphors of Life in Christ

While the techniques of mapping and drawing elements in nature are used in secular educational settings to encourage children to look hard and learn more about nature, we in Christian formation programs have the opportunity to open up nature as a book of metaphors for our lives in Christ. Nature can be an incarnate, visible, touch-able teaching tool to show us how the Body of Christ works.

Think about a watershed. All elements of nature are dependent upon water, a symbol of the Holy Spirit. All water leads, ultimately, to one river or lake, incorporating the water from all over the watershed. All elements of nature interact together, forming a living, breathing, area that nourishes and feeds those creatures and plants that inhabit it. Like the Body of Christ, the parts of the whole may seem small and insignificant in and of themselves, but each part contributes to the health of the whole.

Moving to a larger model, the entire earth is like the Body of Christ. The wind and air blows over and around us all, affecting every single one of us. Water unites us as well.

What we dump or pour into water in one part of the earth affects other parts of the earth. One unhealthy part of the earth can make the entire planet unhealthy. If we want a healthy earth, it matters what we do in our own little part of it.

Think also about a single flower. The flower is unique and beautiful. It blossoms in its own time and in its own place. It is a miracle to behold. Like each unique person, a single flower can be similar to others like it, but it is nevertheless a unique creation inhabiting a specific time and space.

The flower produces seeds, and seeds are the critical to future growth, both of the plant and of life on earth. Seeds are important. And so are our young people. If we want to care for God's creation, one of our most critical missions is to introduce love and care of the earth to young people, the seeds of our future.

Using Your Church and Grounds to Teach Creation Care

Research has shown that the very best way to cultivate environmentalism in young people is, simply, to get them outdoors. For faith-based creation care as well, environmental education is best taught by allowing young people to immerse themselves in nature and experience the wonders of God's creation first hand. Many of these experiences might come about by simply moving a worship service, youth group meeting, or Sunday School class outdoors. If your church is willing to make an more concerted effort to embrace creation care, you might also use the church building and grounds as an important part of your formation program.

These experiences may also take place in a forest, alongside a lake, in a garden, in an urban park, or even in an indoor garden or greenhouse. The land itself can be an important part of your teaching team, providing young people with a learning environment to explore nature, practice spiritual disciplines, and explore important issues of creation care – all while having fun and staying safe. The everyday miracles of nature are free, marvelous tools for spiritual and environmental formation.

Play Areas and Classrooms

For elementary school-age children, free play time is an essential part of child development. During camp, time on a high quality playground will give children time to unwind, freely socialize, and just have fun. An important element of play is use of **"loose objects"** – items which can be freely arranged and re-arranged, manipulated, moved, and used freely for imaginative play. In outdoor settings, these "loose objects" might include sticks, pinecones, piles of leaves, logs, or rocks. **Water** is also a popular element of play for children, so a small stream or manmade re-circulating water feature would likely be a much-used area of play and creative fun.

Outdoor classrooms are a terrific addition to church facilities and can be used for worship, classes, adult and teen meetings, and a wide variety of other special events. An attractive outdoor space may also serve as a focal point for your faith community and will say a lot about what your faith community sees as a priority. Seating for outdoor (and indoor) classrooms is best arranged in circles, so that everyone has a good view of the presentation or focal point. (You will likely find that children pay better attention when seated in a circle, as well.) Natural materials, such as wooden benches, usually blend best with the surrounding environment. A roof or other covering of your outdoor classroom will protect against strong sunlight and make your space useable during rainstorms. Easily washable flooring – or mulch – will allow teachers to demonstrate gardening techniques or make other messy presentations without fear of damaging your classroom.

Gardens are also wonderful teaching spaces. Children and youth may learn first-hand where food comes from in a **kitchen garden**, along with the challenges of watering, weeding, planting, and harvesting. For additional lessons in sustainability, a compost bin and program of recycling kitchen scraps are excellent tools to both teach youth and reduce food and waste costs. Ornamental **flower gardens** are also excellent tools giving children a place for quiet time in nature to listen to God and experience the beauty and delicacy and creation. Presentation of scripture based on nature and agricultural issues would take on new and infinitely deeper meaning if an actual grape vine, a mustard plant, a fig tree, or a wheat crop is used in the lesson itself.

If adding or retrofitting your grounds to include an outdoor classroom is not a possibility (due to budget or space obstacles), there are still ways any church can make its facilities more in tune with creation care. Just add plants.

Any indoor space can be enlivened and enriched for environmental education, and usually at a relatively small cost.

Adding potted plants to your educational space gives young people a small piece of God's creation to care for and to use as a focus of wonder and of learning. Ask parish families to share cut flowers from yards and gardens to cut down costs and to invite participation in your program. The act of watering plants and taking responsibility for them will become an experiential lesson in environmental stewardship. If your plants die from lack of water, it's a teachable lesson in the importance of clean water for living things. If we don't take care of our environment, we lose it.

Going Off the Grid (and Beyond the Church Yard)

If your organization has access to a number of acres of land for your camp or environmental education program, you are blessed indeed – and able to provide a good variety of teaching venues for use by young people. If your church owns land that is currently undeveloped, this can be a huge asset for environmental education. Wilderness and semi-wilderness areas are terrific venues for offering spiritual retreats, trails for contemplative walks, and just room to experience nature in the raw. Many children now live in urban or suburban settings where they simply do not have an opportunity to experience areas of wilderness. Access to forests and undeveloped or lightly developed land is a gift churches can give to their communities.

When offering wild space to children and youth, you will want to set boundaries in which children may explore the area safely and comfortably. By assigning teachers or other adult volunteers to keep an eye on a particular quadrant or specified area, children, their parents, and your staff will feel secure in using the site. Providing walking trails which circle back to a supervised and secure location will also help children feel more secure in exploring nature in the wild. Keeping a first aid kit and a phone on hand to deal with any accidents, cuts, scrapes, or other medical problems will also make everyone feel more confident in spending time outdoors.

As good stewards of our resources, we might look at resource in our communities for resources that may be used for free or at low cost. If your organization or program does not have good outdoor space for use with young people, you might consider holding your program in one of these venues:

- **Local or state parks:** Many cities and states offer parks with hiking or walking trails, picnic areas for meals and group meetings, and perhaps even playground or swimming facilities. Use of these parks may encourage further use by families of your participants.

- **Family farms or wilderness areas**: Families affiliated with your program or organization may be willing to share their farm or large outdoor space for a youth program.

- **Schools, universities, or corporations:** During the summer, schools may be willing to host your program. Likewise, corporations or other private organizations may have facilities available for use for a fee.

Acknowledgements

These curriculum resources have been made possible by a Mark 5 of Mission Fellowship grant by The Episcopal Church. I am tremendously grateful to The Episcopal Church for supporting my work through this fellowship. I am very grateful to The Rev. Canon Mark Stevenson, Jayce Hafner, and Chris Sikkema of the Justice & Advocacy staff of The Episcopal Church for their support, guidance, and wisdom throughout this fellowship. I am also grateful to my colleagues The Rev. Sarah Monroe, The Rev. Susan Heath, and Sarah Nolan for their friendship and support as we shared thoughts on our respective Justice & Advocacy Fellowships. I very much appreciate support for my application to this fellowship from Dorothy Linthicum of Virginia Theological Seminary and from The Rev. Dr. Jerome Berryman of the Godly Play Foundation.

Several Episcopal groups participated in this fellowship by trying out pieces of this curriculum in draft form and by giving me feedback afterwards. I am grateful to Emmanuel Episcopal Church in Greenwood, Virginia and their Director of Christian Education, Cathy Boyd and rector, The Rev. Christopher Garcia; to Grace Point Camp & Conference Center in the Diocese of East Tennessee and its Director, the Rev. Brad Jones; to the Rev. John Mark Wiggers of St. James Episcopal Church in Knoxville; to Church of the Ascension, Episcopal, in Knoxville and its Director of Children's Ministries, Megan Alden and to its Priest in Charge, the Rev. Rob Gieselmann; to Day Pritchartt, Family Minister of Saint Andrews Episcopal Church in Arlington, Virginia; and to the Diocese of East Tennessee and Episcopal School of Knoxville for allowing me to do such good work with Reading Camp Knoxville.

I am thankful for all the children, youth, and adults who used these resources during the summer and fall of 2015 while attending their VBS, camp programs, retreats, or Sunday School classes. It was truly a pleasure to work with all of you.

I am grateful to the University of Tennessee Gardens in Knoxville for providing a rich and wide-ranging program of hands-on workshops on many of the nature-based crafts and activities described in this book. I thoroughly enjoyed all these classes, along with quiet time spent in the UT Gardens themselves as I reflected on the design of this curriculum and got to experience terrific outdoor teaching spaces.

I am particularly grateful to my son Jack for gamely trying out many of the activities and lessons in this book (at times unaware that he did so) and for patiently and articulately giving his mom feedback and suggestions for this work. Finally, I am incredibly thankful for the guidance, support, encouragement, and wisdom of my husband, Tom, who taught me much of what I know about gardening and the natural world…and who moved me out to the country.

About the Author

Cynthia Coe is a 2014-16 Environmental Stewardship Fellow of the Episcopal Church. A graduate of Virginia Theological Seminary, she developed The Abundant Life Garden Project® and other educational resources for Episcopal Relief & Development. She is a former Director of Children's Ministries of Church of the Ascension in Knoxville, Tennessee and the author of *Christian Nurture in the Twenty-First Century: A New Vision for Christian Formation.* She is the mother of three children and lives on a farm in Knox County, Tennessee.

Also by Cynthia Coe:

Christian Nurture in the Twenty-First Century: A New Vision for Christian Formation (2015)

Wild Faith: A Creation Care Curriculum For Youth (2016)

Resources for Teaching

and Studying Creation Care

This is a selected list of books and resources used in the development of this curriculum and recommended for further information, inspiration, and study:

<u>Books for Children and Youth</u>

Mel Bartholomew, *Square Foot Gardening with Kids* (Cool Springs Press, 2014).

Stefan & Beverley Buczacki, *Young Gardener* (Frances Lincoln Children's Books, 2006).

HRH The Prince of Wales, *Harmony: A Vision for Our Future* (HarperCollins, 2010).

Michael Pollan, *Food Rules: An Eater's Manual – Illustrated Edition* with art by Maira Kalman (Penguin Books, 2011).

Michael Pollan, *Young Readers Edition: The Omnivore's Dilemma* (Dial Books for Young Readers/Penguin Group, 2009).

<u>Books and Resources for Teachers:</u>

Abundant Life Garden Project® resources from Episcopal Relief & Development. (Episcopal Relief & Development, 2011) <u>www.episcopalrelief.org/children</u>

Herbert W. Broda, *Moving the Classroom Outdoors: Schoolyard-Enhanced Learning in Action* (Stenhouse Publishers, 2011).

Get-to-know.org (Wild Neighbours Society, British Columbia, Canada. www.get-to-know.org/education/)

Karen Liebriech, Jutta Wagner, and Annette Wendland, *The Family Kitchen Garden* (Timber Press, 2009).

Richard Louv, *Last Child in the Woods: Saving Our Children from Nature-Deficit Disorder* (Algonquin Books of Chapel Hill, 2008).

Lisa Miller, Ph.D. with Teresa Barker, *The Spiritual Child: The New Science on Parenting for Health and Lifelong Thriving* (St. Martin's Press, 2015).

David Sobel, *Childhood and Nature: Design Principles for Educators* (Stenhouse Publishers, 2008).

Aline D. Wolf, *Nurturing the Spirit in Non-Sectarian Classrooms*. Available at www.montessoriservices.com.

Books for Further Study by Adults:

Theology and Spirituality:

Jennifer R. Ayres, *Good Food: Grounded Practical Theology* (Baylor University Press, 2013).

Fred Bahnson and Norman Wirzba, *Making Peace with the Land: God's Call to Reconcile with Creation* (Intervarsity Press, 2012).

Diana Butler Bass, *Grounded: Finding God in the World, A Spiritual Revolution* (HarperOne, 2015)

Elizabeth T. Groppe, *Eating & Drinking* (Fortress Press, 2011)

James Jones, *Jesus and the Earth* (SPCK, 2003).

L. Shannon Jung, *Sharing Food: Christian Practices for Enjoyment* (Fortress Press, 2006)

Belden C. Lane , *Backpacking With the Saints* (Oxford University Press, 2015)

Sallie McFague, *Super, Natural Christians* (Fortress Press, 1997).

Sallie McFague, *Life Abundant* (Fortress Press, 2001).

Michael Schut with Wendell Berry, Thomas Moore, Elizabeth Johnson, John Robbins & others, *Food & Faith: Justice, Joy and Daily Bread* (Morehouse Publishing, 2009)

Claire Thompson, *Mindfulness & the Natural World: Bringing our Awareness Back to Nature* (Metro Books, 2013).

Fred Van Dyke, David C. Mahan, Joseph K. Sheldon, & Raymond H. Brand, *Redeeming Creation: The Biblical Basis for Environmental Stewardship* (Intervarsity Press: 1996)

Ed. Tripp York and Andy Alexis-Baker, *A Faith Encompassing All Creation* (Cascade Books, 2014).

Secular Books Inviting Reflection and Discussion:

Jane Goodall, *Reason for Hope: A Spiritual Journey* (Grand Central Publishing/Hachette Book Group, 2003).

HRH The Prince of Wales, *Harmony: A New Way of Looking at our World* (HarperCollins, 2012).

Barbara Kingsolver, *Animal, Vegetable, Miracle: A Year of Food Life* (HarperCollins, 2008).

Barbara Kingsolver, *Flight Behavior* (HarperCollins, 2012).

Barbara Kingsolver, *Prodigal Summer* (HarperCollins, 2000).

Richard Louv, *The Nature Principle: Reconnecting with Life in a Virtual Age* (Algonquin Books of Chapel Hill, 2012).

Michael Pollan, *The Omnivore's Dilemma* (Penguin, 2007).

Debra Prinzing, *The 50 Mile Bouquet: Seasonal, Local and Sustainable Flowers* (St. Lynn's Press, 2012)

Tricia Shapiro, *Mountain Justice: Homegrown Resistance to Mountaintop Removal, For the Future of Us All* (AK Press, 2010).

Amy Stewart, *Flower Confidential: The Good, the Bad, and the Beautiful* (Algonquin Books of Chapel Hill, 2007).

Years of Living Dangerously. (Showtime, 2015)
www.sho.com/sho/years-of-living-dangerously/home

Made in the USA
San Bernardino, CA
18 April 2016